# Embroidery & Architecture

# Embroidery & Architecture

## Jan Messent

B. T. Batsford Ltd  London

# Acknowledgment

I would like to acknowledge, with thanks, the kind help and willing co-operation of those who have allowed me to use their work to illustrate this book; their generosity is much appreciated. Special thanks are due to my friend Vincent Morris who developed and printed my photographs with great skill, and who, to my benefit, showed much interest in the whole project. Valerie Campbell-Harding was, as always, a great and valuable asset and unselfish lender of ideas and material, and to her I owe much.

Belinda Baker, my editor, has been a joy to work with—kind, thorough and helpful. My sincere thanks to her.

To my loving and undemanding family, my thanks for helping me through the past year with their support and understanding.

© Jan Messent 1985

First published 1985

ISBN 0 7134 3703 0

Printed in Great Britain by
Anchor Brendon Ltd, Tiptree, Essex
for the publishers
B T Batsford Limited
4 Fitzhardinge Street
London W1H 0AH

# Contents

Acknowledgment  4

Introduction  7
A Brief Survey  9
Sources of Design  18
Styles of Design  20
Word Associations as Ideas for Design  23
Perspective and Depth  24
Scale  26
Some Simple Ways of Making a Design  27
Plans  38
The Materials of Architecture  43
Doors and Arches  59
Windows  76
Stairs and Steps  88
Decoration  93
Spires, Towers and Domes  116
Architecture in the Environment  122
Ruins  134
Nature Takes Over  139

Bibliography  142
Suppliers  143
Index  144

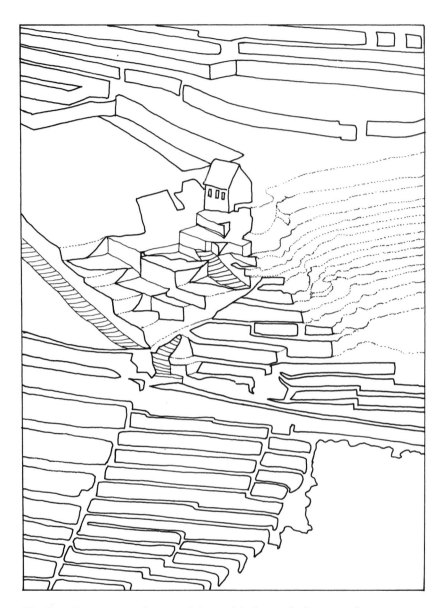

The lines drawn over a photograph have picked up only the areas of contrast between the shadows and the sunlit shapes. All suggestions of texture have been ignored as it was the pattern of terraces and ruins which arrested the attention. The spaces are an essential part of the design

# Introduction

This is the author's fourth source book of design ideas for embroiderers, following on after ancient and primitive designs, the world of nature and animals.

In a book of ideas, it would be out of place to attempt at the same time to explain how to embroider; there are many excellent books on embroidery techniques which will give you a working knowledge of the ways in which the ideas shown here may be used, and the author recommends that students familiarize themselves with as many embroidery techniques as possible to provide a greater vocabulary by which to express ideas. At the same time, I sincerely hope that students of other crafts may find this book useful in their search for inspiration—jewellers, sculptors, wood-carvers, painters and graphic-artists, to mention only a few.

Embroidery techniques have been mentioned only loosely where it is thought that a design lends itself particularly well to a certain technique, although these are merely suggestions. Most designs may be adapted in a variety of ways and it is worthwhile experimenting to find the best way of interpreting an idea before starting a full-scale piece, even to the extent of trying out part of the design in different techniques. (See figs 43–45.)

Although many of the drawings show architecture which you may partly recognize, in most cases they have not been identified in the captions because my presentation of them as designs has meant that they have had to be changed, and in some cases my artist's licence has run amok! Little bits of other buildings, or decoration, may have been grafted on, and unnecessary parts excluded all in the name of design, but I hope this will help to show how things may be seen more simply and in a less daunting light. One can take more liberties with designs from architecture than with those from many other sources (animals and plants, for instance) as they are composed of so many parts with which one may juggle, resulting in an acceptable mixture of elements which disturbs no-one by its new non-functional role, unlike animal designs which will withstand only so much juggling and no more.

It is almost impossible to keep the many facets of architectural design in separate compartments, as they overlap each other considerably. Pattern is found in every aspect of the subject, as is texture, and shape, so the subject headings are quite elastic and only serve to point out the many features of inspiration, and not to pinpoint them too specifically. Modern buildings will be found to be just as decorative as older ones, especially to those interested in abstract design; often their simpler shapes make them more suitable for certain embroidery techniques than older, more highly-decorated buildings. Nature encroaches on old and new buildings alike and has been given a little compartment of its own even though it makes frequent appearances throughout the other sections.

In any book covering such a vast subject, it is inevitable that some things will be left out which one may expect to find—watermills, Dutch town-houses, Japanese, Chinese and Indian architecture—the list is great. Some of these places were too far away for me to photograph, some were too difficult for me to draw, and for some it was hard to find suitable pictures. However, maybe there are enough ideas here to whet the appetite of embroiderers, who will, I hope, gain as much pleasure from using the material as I have done in preparing it.

A large mosaic basin (now in the Victoria and Albert Museum, London) showing rich pattern in a series of arches

# A Brief Survey

Fashions and requirements move forward with the changes in the structure of society. A study of the history of embroidery shows clearly that each major change in style and subject is linked to other changes such as social and religious attitudes.

Embroidery throughout the centuries has been influenced, like most other things, by economic necessity, world events, social considerations or practical reasons. This can be simply illustrated by the use of embroidered wall-hangings instead of the genuine costly tapestries which were used to insulate large rooms in the seventeenth century, and the adoption of Chinese-style motifs after new links were made with China and India in the late seventeenth and early eighteenth centuries. The decorative bed-hangings in large houses not only kept out draughts but demonstrated the wealth of the affluent occupants, unlike the practical and beautiful patchwork quilts of the New World Americans, which were made at home from small scraps of used fabric and so cost comparatively little.

Changes of need also introduced differences of style and technique; the skill involved was another factor, not only among professionals who would often seek a quicker but technically less acceptable method to achieve a more productive line, but also among amateur embroiderers world-wide whose limitations have had a positive effect upon style and subject matter. Samplers made by young girls are an example of this, as are the popular embroidery kits of today.

In this way fashions in subject matter take their turn according to the era, its needs and connections. An almost exclusive emphasis on ecclesiastical figures and heraldic devices in the early Middle Ages was followed by stylized naturalistic forms and patterns, based on the classical lines popular throughout the Renaissance in Europe. The Elizabethan preoccupation with gardens and the details of nature had its inescapable effect on everything embroidered at that time, just as at *this* time modern embroiderers are finding ways in which to express deeply felt philosophies about the meaning and quality of life and existence, about world-wide problems and personal beliefs. It need hardly be mentioned that these trends have developed since links with every part of the globe have been encouraged and concern for those less fortunate than others is now expressed in every medium available to us.

It is only natural that associated design sources should have some influence on each other: manuscripts, sculpture in stone and wood, painting, metalwork and textiles have all made use of the same designs and patterns at one time or another, each adapting them in its own way to suit the medium. Some of the earliest English embroideries share the style of the stone and wood carvings of the eleventh and twelfth centuries seen in Romanesque and Gothic buildings all over Europe (fig. 1), taking the form of architectural settings with figures surrounded by turreted castles and arched canopies to emphasize their importance (figs 3, 4 and 5). Manuscripts of this time show similar figures enclosed by arches, painted in the same detailed and decorative style.

At the same time as the much-loved theme of nature was taking its course in Elizabethan England, embroiderers were also turning their attention to large wall- and bed-hangings resembling in scale and subject the beautiful pictorial tapestries of France and Germany. As links with these countries were forged and design influences filtered in, the idea of depicting stories from the Bible and ancient mythology caught hold. As in other artistic spheres the subjects were treated in an entirely new and typically English manner; Biblical figures were dressed in contemporary clothes and moved among the beautiful classical colonnades, pillars, domed temples and marble fountains of Renaissance Italy. Pattern-books of architecture were avidly sought by craftsmen of all kinds for the newest ideas from Europe which were embroidered onto the bed-hangings of those who could afford them. For those who, for various reasons, were less influenced by the new styles of design, rural scenes of contemporary English life were lovingly worked on large-scale objects such as the Bradford Table Carpet (figs 6 and 7) which may have been household labours of love rather than professional undertakings. The particular example mentioned shows churches, farmhouses, manor houses and cottages, as well as windmills and watermills, all typical of the period and delightfully real. Some enterprising and forceful characters such as the Countess of Shrewsbury (Bess of Hardwick), actually designed their own embroideries and also took part in the execution of them. The inventory of Hardwick Hall (Bess's new home) lists numerous examples of wall-hangings and long cushions with scenes from mythology, and also a unique one: 'an other long quition [cushion] of nedleworke of the platt [plan] of Chatesworth house with grene red and yellowe silke frenge buttons of Carnation silke and silver & lyned with white grene and yellowe cloth of silver ...' indicating that she apparently also thought a ground plan decorative enough to form a design on a cushion.

The appreciation of pictorial embroidery continued throughout the seventeenth century (fig. 8) and flourished briefly in the three-dimensional stumpwork used to decorate boxes and small cabinets, mirror-frames and book covers. On these may be seen highly padded and fanciful buildings in the distance, clustered on top of little mounds (fig. 9). Indian and Chinese influences were at work, however, on the embroidery designs of mid-seventeenth century crewel-work, showing oriental houses, birds and animals among luscious foliage (fig. 11), and later in the century the fashionable Chinese idiom was even more apparent in the pagodas, bridges, pavilions and willows executed in silks on coverlets (fig. 12). Known as 'Chinoiserie', this influence extended to many other facets of interior decoration.

Samplers, which had originally been records of patterns and exercises for amateur needlewomen, gradually underwent a change and became instead pictorial records of personal data and favourite motifs, often in cross stitch only, usually made by young girls. Favourite subjects very often included a house which may, I suggest, have been part real and part fanciful, and often occupied the most important position on the sampler around which other motifs were scattered. Some of these 'house samplers' (figs 14–17) are indeed delightful, and evoke a real feeling of closeness to the little worker who had found such a personal means of expression in a world where this was not generally encouraged among young people.

It will be seen that buildings featured only as a general part of pictorial embroidery and composite patchwork designs, as additions to themes concerned mainly with figures and flowers. Only rarely were buildings used as the central theme; indeed in later centuries they seem to have been almost totally excluded in favour of floral designs such as those of William Morris and Jessie Newbery. It is only in comparatively recent times that the beauty and diversity of buildings as a design source has been exploited, as the whole field of art has widened to include everything as potential design material rather than slavishly following the fashion. Although it is still possible nowadays to identify works as belonging to this or that era, these trends are of shorter duration and of a more exploratory nature both in subject matter and technique.

Embroidery is at last taking its rightful place among other art forms and is seen now in its unique role as a means of expression, not merely as a decoration on some otherwise unremarkable household object. As in painting, embroiderers are now free to develop their own recognizable styles using any technique or subject, and, as a result, many works are instantly attributable to a particular embroiderer. Students of embroidery are encouraged to search for new material rather than to follow paths already trodden, in exact opposition to previous times. The vast design source of architecture has at last been tapped and discovered to be one of the largest, most decorative and most rewarding of all. Men design buildings to please both themselves and others, providing us with ready-made ideas for designs, not always in their entirety, but sufficient to trigger off ideas of colour, texture, pattern or shape. We have to learn to look for these ideas and translate them into our own media, and whether we live in town, city, village or even in total isolation, the material for design is always with us.

**1** Detail drawn from a Romanesque stone carving now in the Victoria and Albert Museum, London, showing the same style of arched canopy used to enclose figures as those seen in embroideries of this period

**2** Italian stone carving from the same period, showing arches and towers

**3** Building detail from the Bayeux Tapestry (English, twelfth century). Embroidery worked in wool on linen

**4** Detail of arches and towers from the back of a mid-thirteenth-century Austrian chasuble

**5** Detail from an English chasuble orphrey of 1390–1420, embroidered on linen in coloured silks and metal threads. It forms part of an idealized version of the structure surrounding the Nativity

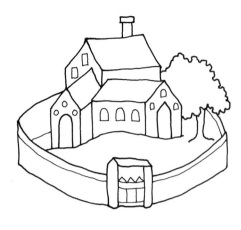

**6, 7** Two details from the Bradford table carpet made in England during the late sixteenth century

**8** A cluster of buildings taken from an embroidered picture of the seventeenth century, worked in silk and metal threads

**9** Detail from a mid-seventeenth-century picture of Abraham and Hagar, worked in raised stitches over padding. Like many of the other sections of the embroidery, this was made separately and applied to the satin background

**10** A town seen in the distance, from a picture (or long cushion cover) of Abraham and the Angels, worked in the mid-seventeenth century in tent stitch on canvas

**11** Detail of a Chinoiserie design on a crewel-work curtain of 1680

15

**12** Detail of pagodas in the Chinoiserie style, worked on a silk coverlet in silk threads by Sarah Thurstone in 1694

**14** A house from an English cross-stitch sampler of 1780

**13** A windmill from an English cross-stitch sampler of 1789

**15** A more impressive English manor house from an English cross-stitch sampler of 1800.

**16** An American house from a nineteenth-century sampler, showing details of patterned brickwork, multiple gables and chimneys

**17** A house from an eighteenth-century
Dutch sampler worked in cross stitch

**18** A detail from a Danish sampler of 1798.
This delightful scene shows a village from
a distance, with the church and windmill.
The layered hillocks in the foreground
appear to be sand-dunes

# Sources of Design

Architecture is one of the most attractive subjects to embroiderers not only because the materials of buildings are all around us but also because designs may easily be made from the simplest shapes of our imagination. We drew houses as soon as we learnt to recognize their shapes, and as small children we learned to appreciate the patterns of the buildings we drew. Those who have not drawn for many years need not feel that their skills with a pencil are inadequate, as buildings have already been designed by architects and all *we* have to do is to adapt them a little and add a few ideas of our own.

Doors and windows, decoration on ceilings and columns, shapes of staircases and woodwork provide attractive indoor themes on which to base an embroidery design, even for the housebound. Many ideas may be found in books, for while it is always exciting to see buildings at first-hand this is by no means possible for many of us. Photographs provide a valuable record of parts of buildings we could not have seen even if we had been there ourselves. Detailed studies are often made more successfully from photographs of buildings than in any other way, presenting a two-dimensional view which is easier for us to translate.

There are, of course, many ideas to be found in our own local towns and countryside, and embroiderers are encouraged to stand and look at the upper parts of buildings which they may have passed many times already without noticing. Modern shop-fittings are often added to the lower storeys while the old parts of the upper storeys remain intact, and unnoticed carved stonework or fancy brickwork, decorated gables and complicated tile patterns are there above our heads (fig. 19). One of the best times to stand and stare is on a Sunday when there are fewer people and cars; take a sketch book or camera to make a record of these details for your future use. They may be used in the context of a design based on buildings, or in isolation as a decoration, or as the basis of an abstract design.

**19** Decoration on the upper storeys of shops in Norwich

# Styles of Design

It is remarkably easy, while exploring architectural shapes, to find examples of the various styles of design, and while I am not in favour of keeping things in pigeonholes for long, it may help to explain these basic categories in order to make looking more fun and more interesting.

## 1 Symbolic (fig. 20)

The photograph shows a large sculpture, outside a newspaper building in Norwich, of large metallic spheres being pressed by rectangular blocks of stone. It would seem (to me) to be a play on the word 'press' and may even suggest other associated words such as distortion, suppression and freedom. Symbolism in design is a way of suggesting ideas in a visual way by means of the simplest possible shapes, whether two- or three-dimensional.

**20** Stone and metal sculpture, Norwich

## 2 Abstract (fig. 21)

The winged triangular shapes of the Sydney Opera House in Australia are shown here. The details which identify it as a building have been left out of this drawing, making it look like an arrangement of shapes and nothing more. An abstract design need not be identifiable as anything in particular, but relies on a satisfying arrangement of shapes and tones.

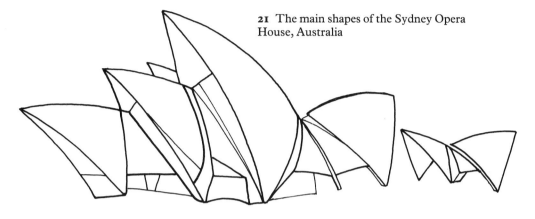

**21** The main shapes of the Sydney Opera House, Australia

## 3 Stylized (fig. 22)

The acanthus leaves on top of these plaster columns are recognizable as leaves but look too rigid and formal to be natural. They are therefore called 'stylized', which is a way of presenting material in a highly decorative style while still retaining its identity.

**22** Plaster columns, Halifax Teachers' Centre

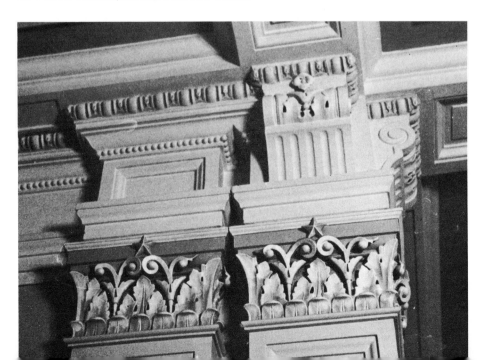

## 4 Naturalistic (Fig. 23)

The acanthus leaves on this stone carving look more real and could therefore be called 'naturalistic'. Anything which is presented as it is actually seen comes under this heading, even if details have been altered here and there.

**23** Carved stone corbels on the outside of a church in Reading

The style which you choose will depend partly upon your personal preference, the source of your idea and the technique you wish to use, but ideas can be adapted to result in a combination of these styles.

# Word Associations as Ideas for Design

As you have seen in fig. 20, the association of words and visual ideas can produce some very interesting results. Words with an architectural meaning abound in our everyday language, some literal and others metaphorical. Some of these words are listed below in the hope that they will stimulate the imagination towards the development of a positive theme for a design. Some words have *two* literal interpretations as well as metaphorical ones.

| | | | |
|---|---|---|---|
| conservatory | quarters | houseroom | perch |
| extension | headquarters | dolls' house | hutch |
| accommodation | precinct | coffee house | cage |
| For Sale | courtyard | tea house | dog-house |
| To Let | quadrangle | country seat | workhouse |
| freehold | compound | township | summer house |
| leasehold | hole & corner | lodge | glass house |
| settlement | haunt | squatter | greenhouse |
| anchorage | store | pigeon-hole | winter palace |
| habitation | household | roost | boat house |

# Perspective and Depth

If your draughtsmanship is not yet adequate to cope with such things as angles and vanishing points, then forget perspective altogether and draw your buildings in two dimensions, presenting only one side of a building and ignoring the rest.

Fig. 24 shows a photograph of a row of houses taken at an angle. The sketch opposite this (fig. 27) shows how this has been simplified and the angle of view changed so that the problem of perspective has been eliminated altogether except for the sign which would disappear if seen from the front. The details of the door on the left had to be guessed at, but a little research would provide this kind of information, and the gate on the right is shown closed to provide an extra decorative feature.

**24** A row of houses in Norwich, seen at an angle

25

26

The suggestion of depth adds an extra dimension to a design. If you wish to assist the eye to focus on a certain area, one way is to deepen the tones nearest the viewer and allow them to become paler towards the distance. This may be tried the other way round too, for a different effect (figs 25, 26).

**27** A sketch drawn from the previous photograph, seen from a different viewpoint

# Scale

Our own observations tell us the relative sizes of objects; we know that buildings are large compared to people and bushes, for instance, but we also know that the size of even large buildings appears to diminish as we move away from them. This illusion can make relatively small things appear much greater in relation to a distant view of a building, an effect which has great value to a designer as can be seen in the two examples in figs 28 and 29.

It is worth mentioning here that a two- and three-dimensional approach may be used on the same design. In fig. 29 the balustrade is left flat with no attempt to suggest its solidity, while the scene beyond is quite naturalistic. It could just as effectively have been shown the other way round.

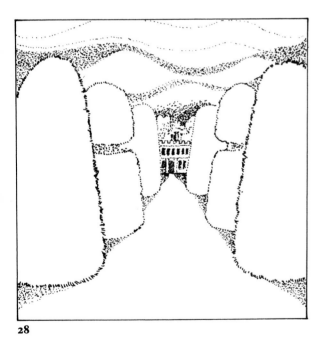

28

29

# Some Simple Ways of Making a Design

Designing is by no means always a pencil and paper exercise; there are many other ways of achieving results which are perfect for translation to embroidery. Here are some of the simplest methods which may be used alone or in conjunction with others. More methods are discussed throughout the following chapters.

1 Collect the architectural motifs from 'house samplers', put these all together in one design and translate this into a different technique.

2 On a background of cross stitch, place a small statue of padded calico (quilt the details) to give an impression of high relief.

3 Cut a white card shape of simple balustrades like those seen on stone patios, wrap this with white threads, leaving the corners uncovered, and place across the lower part of a delicately embroidered view of parkland and/or a manor house.

4 Using a colour photograph or small painting of a building, design an area of textured foliage in crunchy embroidery to surround it, encroaching onto the edges of the picture like a frame.

5 As a border to a simple embroidery, devise a pattern of buildings (or patterns *from* buildings) to go around the edge.

6 Cut out a card shape of spectacles or binocular lenses and cover this with fabric or threads. Inside the lens area, place an embroidered view of buildings, windows or doors, perhaps with a figure.

7 Make a frame of log-cabin patchwork for a small photograph or embroidery of buildings.

8 Hardanger embroidery lends itself particularly well to window and door shapes, as it involves areas of rectangular cutwork. Use this idea in conjunction with a small photograph or painting by placing the embroidered window over the top to form a frame.

**9** Cut out shapes of different-coloured paper to make a collage. Re-arrange the shapes to adjust the tones and to experiment with the balance. Fig. 30a shows an example of this method, and fig. 30b shows how the design has been worked in felt using a sewing machine to apply the pieces and to add texture.

**30a** A paper collage of St James the Greater, Leicester, designed by Jennie Parry. (*Photo: V. A. Campbell-Harding*)

**30b** Felt appliqué with machine stitches by Jennie Parry, using the design in the previous illustration. (*Photo: V. A. Campbell-Harding*)

**30c** A blackwork panel of the same design by Jennie Parry

**10** Look closely at small, detailed decorations too, as these make good motifs for repeat patterns which may be used on garments. Fig. 31 shows four of these small motifs which have been repeated to form squares (perhaps for a pocket or cushion design) (fig. 32) and also as a border (fig. 33).

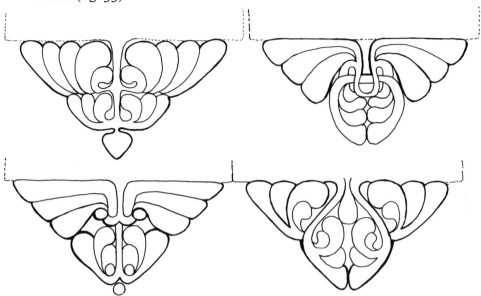

**31** Stone window details from a thirteenth-century church in Annaghdown, Co. Galway, Ireland

**32,33** Square and border repeat patterns based on fig. 31

**11** An abstract design can sometimes be made by cutting a photograph into strips and re-arranging them as in fig. 34. Some of the strips have been turned upside-down, but none is in the original order. Trace over the re-arrangement to obtain a rough idea of the shapes you require (fig. 35), then keep tracing each previous one until you achieve a more balanced design (figs 36 and 37), adding and subtracting parts all the time and ignoring the original photograph during these stages.

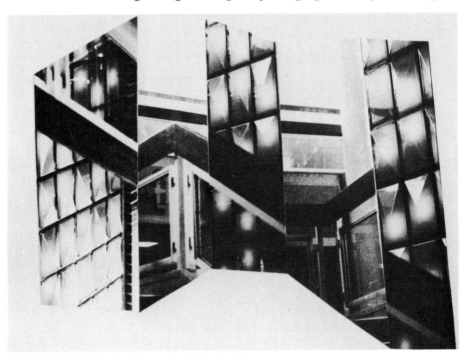

**34** Photograph of a shopping-precinct stairway, cut into five strips and re-arranged

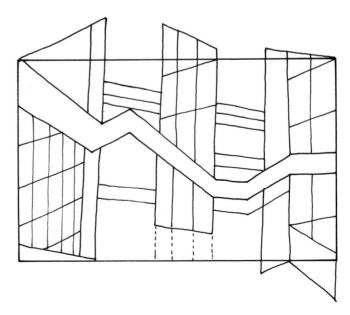

**35** First tracing, made of the most important elements

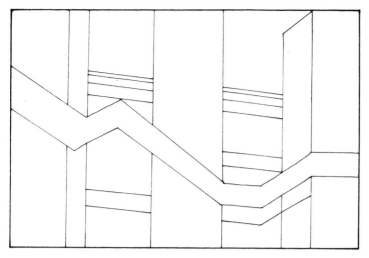

**36** Second tracing, to simplify the design

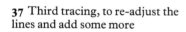
**37** Third tracing, to re-adjust the lines and add some more

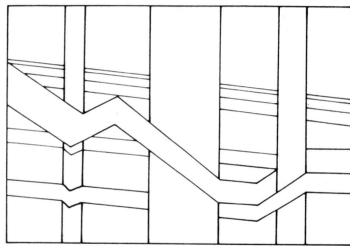

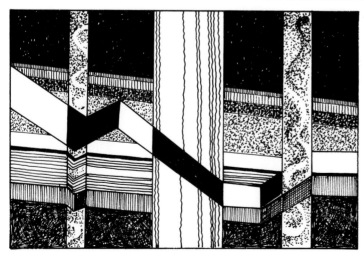

**38** The same design, with added tones and textures

**12** Photographs of highly decorated buildings will provide many patterns which may be isolated as seen in fig. 39. These units can then be used as building blocks to reconstruct a design (fig. 40). Turn the units any way up, simplify or add to them, enlarge or reduce them, then add ideas of your own—a spire, dome or tower.

**39** Part of the tower, highly decorated arches, and windows of Norwich Cathedral

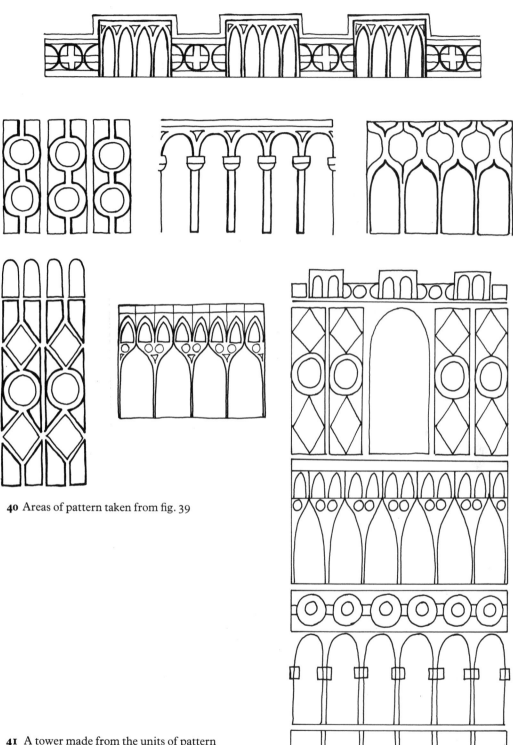

**40** Areas of pattern taken from fig. 39

**41** A tower made from the units of pattern in fig. 40

**13** Make a simple diagram of lines and blocks like the one in fig. 42a and work the design in different ways using the same technique.

**42a,b,c** Diagram and canvaswork by Lyn Hughes

**14** Using a simple design of part of a building, make small samples using different techniques to see which one is most effective.

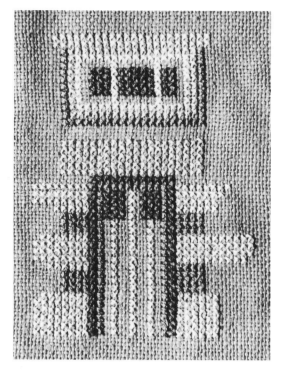

**43** ABOVE LEFT Cross stitch embroidery
**44** ABOVE Shadow quilting

**45** Canvas embroidery

**15** Large, decorative elements seen on buildings are often perfect for embroidery as is the one in fig. 46 designed by the American architect Frank Lloyd Wright. It may be used exactly as it is, or repeated in the various ways shown, in a square format or as a border.

**46** Design in stone by Frank Lloyd-Wright

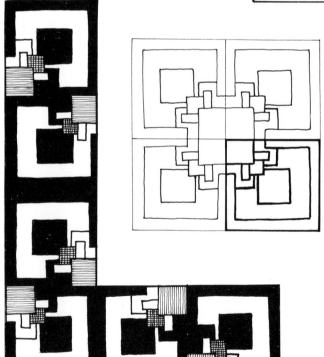

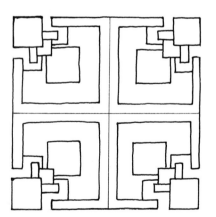

**47, 48, 49** Square and border repeat patterns based on fig. 46

50 House interior

16   Some dolls' houses are extremely decorative and may suggest designs
for a panel showing a simplified cross-section of rooms. This idea may
be extended to make some parts almost three-dimensional and some
detachable.

# Plans

Like aerial views, plans have an almost abstract quality which can be expressed in a wide variety of techniques. They may be further simplified or allowed to retain their original appearance as recognizable plans, though the colours used need bear no relationship to the real ones.

Old photographs and plans showing the countryside and towns as they used to be are easily found; if a series of the same area could be acquired this would make an interesting project for an embroidery design. Books on aerial photography provide spectacular views of towns and villages in many countries which will translate almost immediately into techniques such as patchwork, quilting, couching and counted-thread methods. Hunt in your local library for these; they are usually in the section reserved for large books. Architects' drawings are good sources too, as they are always beautifully drawn in a decorative style useful to the embroiderer, and can usually be easily simplified.

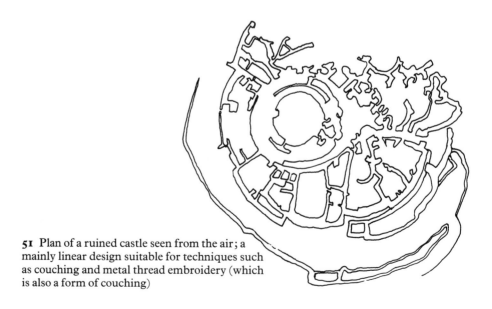

**51** Plan of a ruined castle seen from the air; a mainly linear design suitable for techniques such as couching and metal thread embroidery (which is also a form of couching)

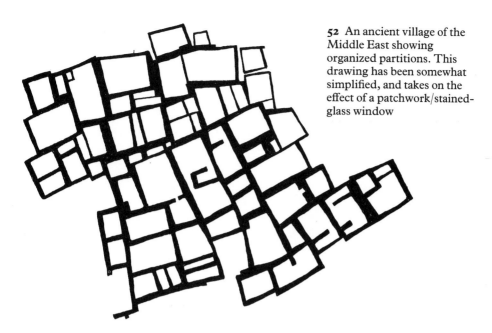

**52** An ancient village of the Middle East showing organized partitions. This drawing has been somewhat simplified, and takes on the effect of a patchwork/stained-glass window

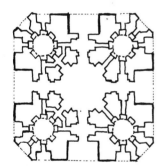

**53** The simplified ground-plan of an Islamic building

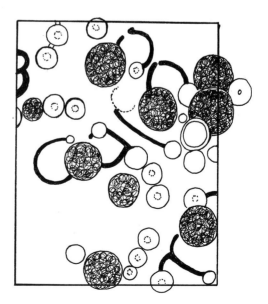

**54** Circular dwellings in an African village showing smaller granaries and enclosing walls

39

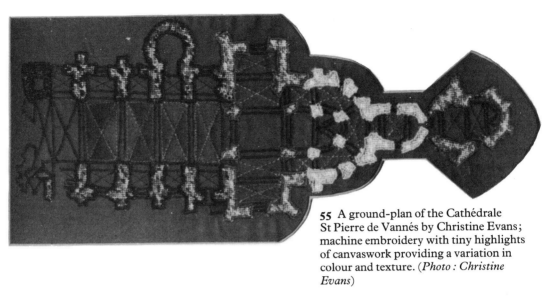

**55** A ground-plan of the Cathédrale St Pierre de Vannés by Christine Evans; machine embroidery with tiny highlights of canvaswork providing a variation in colour and texture. (*Photo: Christine Evans*)

**56** 'Home and Garden'; a small machine- and hand-stitched panel by Christine Evans, based on a ground-plan. In the centre, silk organza pieces are overlaid onto a background of silk. (*Photo: Christine Evans*)

**57** 'Garden and House Plan' by Christine Evans; hand and machine stitchery with applied fabrics and seminole patchwork on silk. (*Photo: Christine Evans*)

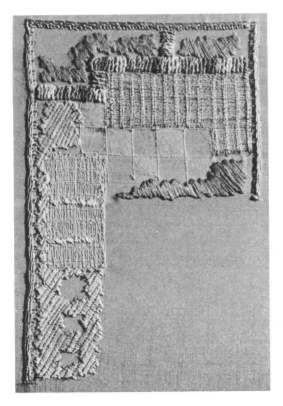

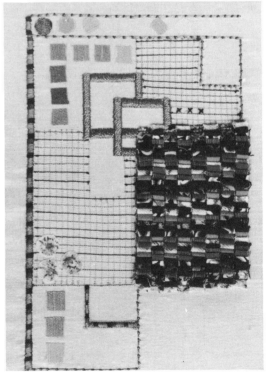

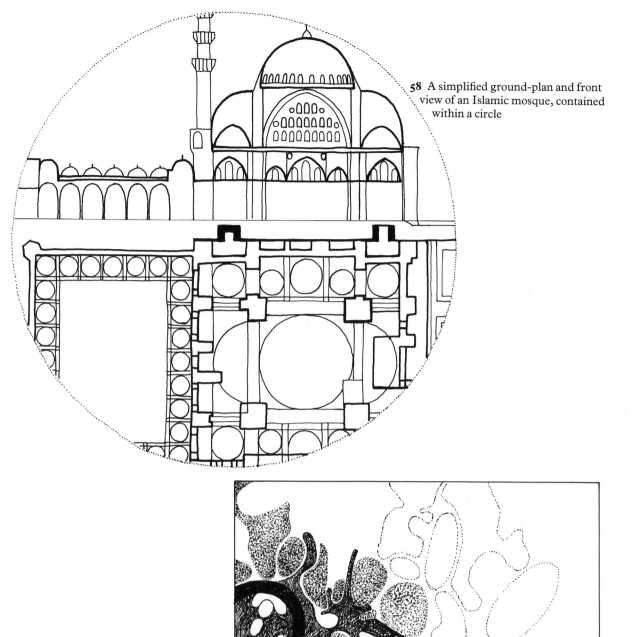

**58** A simplified ground-plan and front view of an Islamic mosque, contained within a circle

**59** A diagrammatic plan of London (upside down) simplified into areas of concentrated industries and other activities

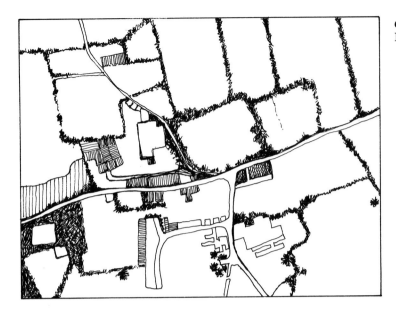

**60a** An aerial view of an English village

**60b** A reconstruction of fig. 60a, now simplified to merge several fields into one, to keep the buildings towards the central cross-roads where most of the interest lies, and to connect the roads into a series of lines which leads the eye in and out of the picture

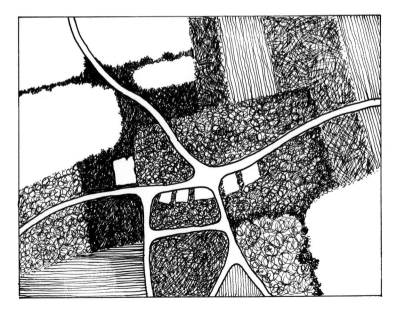

# The Materials of Architecture

Architecture need not necessarily be imagined in terms of complete buildings; the materials used provide many ideas for design, as will be seen in this chapter. One need only visit a builder's yard, a timber merchant, a roofing specialist and a building construction site to get an idea of the range of textures, patterns, colours and shapes of materials. The information you gather can be used as the basis for experimental work in preparation for something larger: a pattern of tiles may inspire a design not related to the original subject at all.

Look carefully at brickwork as you pass by, as the ways in which bricks are laid vary quite considerably. Some old walls, particularly of the Victorian era, are very ornamental and may be made of different-coloured bricks forming a pattern discoloured by time.

Look out, too, for lichen- and moss-covered walls and roofs; the colours and textures may remind you of pads of velvet and lace. A project based on walls, tiles or brickwork patterns would be an excellent one for a student to explore.

Construction sites are particularly fascinating with their networks of scaffolding, sheets of shiny polythene and many different textures: smooth new concrete against heaps of rubble, long lines of wires and cables, lace-like wire grids and shadows of straight-sided buildings falling over uneven ground. Tall cranes and the machinery of building also have their place in design, as do human figures alongside huge constructions, lending scale and focal points to the mechanical scene.

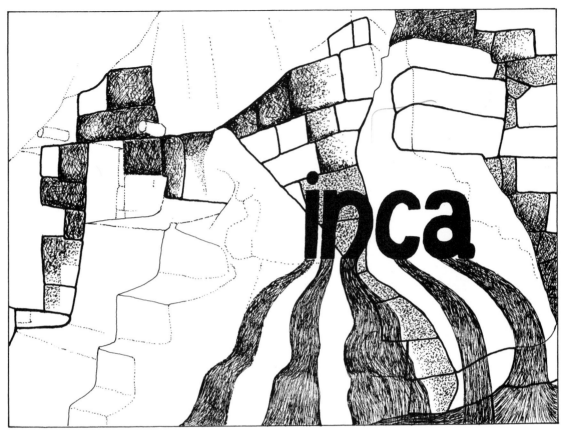

**61** Lettering incorporated into massive stonework forms an interesting design which could be translated into a combination of padded appliqué, quilting and goldwork

**62** An Inca wall showing the perfect fit of the huge stones

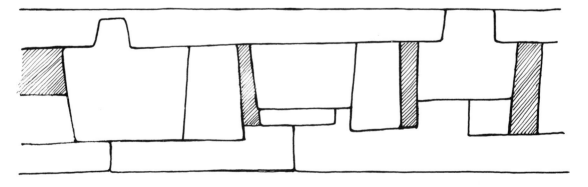

**63** The comparatively rough stonework of an ivy-covered wall-niche at Grantley Hall in Yorkshire

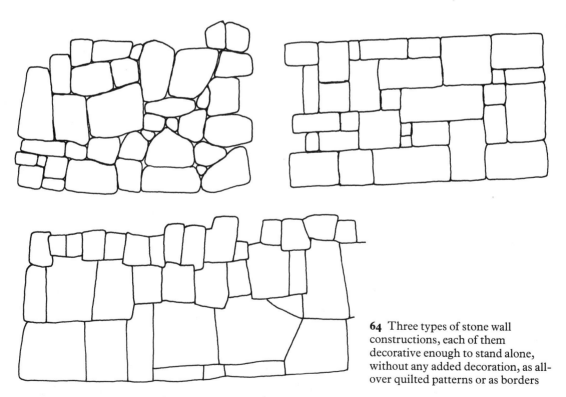

**64** Three types of stone wall constructions, each of them decorative enough to stand alone, without any added decoration, as all-over quilted patterns or as borders

45

**65** The rough wall of a ruin in Norwich

**66** Part of a ruined castle in France showing a pattern of square holes and roughened slabs. (*Photo : V. A. Campbell-Harding*)

46

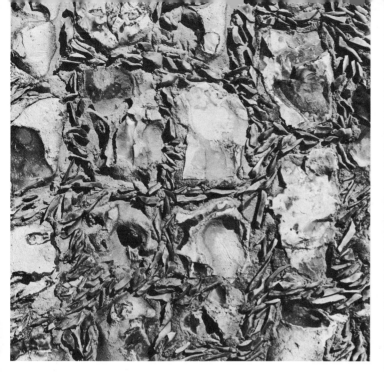

**67** Rough chunks of stone set into cement and surrounded by flints create an almost textile-like appearance of rough rags. (*Photo: V. A. Campbell-Harding*)

**68** A concrete tower-block at the Barbican, London

**69** A section of the castle at Norwich showing several areas of cut stonework fitting together in harmony

70

71    72

OPPOSITE
**70** Cobblestones and raised flower-beds blend together to form patterns of movement, organized and random. Try this effect in embroidery in one technique (as in fig. 71) or in two different ones

**71** Canvas embroidery, organized and random

**72** Stacks of bricks seen in a builder's yard. Note that odd bricks here and there are turned the other way round and that not all of them are the same thickness and texture

**73** A canvas embroidery experiment by Jennie Parry includes braids and beads. This simulates the same kind of organized pattern of bricks as seen in fig. 72. (*Photo: V. A. Campbell-Harding*)

**74** A stack of bricks in a builder's yard

**75** Brickwork patterns vary in different parts of the country and from one country to another. Keep a sketchbook or camera handy to record these patterns, as they are perfect for translation into embroidery. The drawing on the left shows patterns seen on the roof, walls and windows

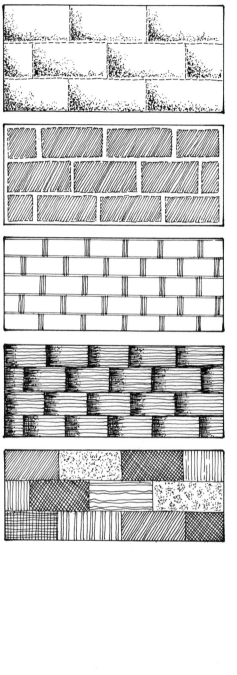

**76** As an exercise, translate a pattern of bricks in five or six different ways. This drawn example shows, from top to bottom, quilting, shadow-quilting, couched ribbon, satin stitch and patchwork

**77** A set of decorative brickwork chimneys at Hampton Court Palace

**78** Old tiles covered with moss and lichen

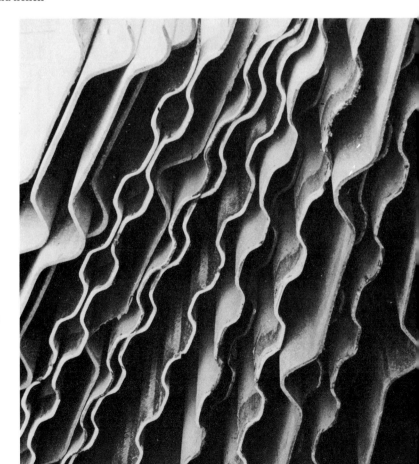

**79** Sheets of roofing material create slightly varying wavy lines in an irregular arrangement, looking rather like couched threads or machine stitching

52

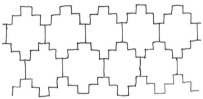

**80** Older houses tend to be far more decorative than modern ones, as when they were built time was not so pressing, and labour was cheaper. The upper part of this house in Norwich is covered with patterns of tiles, bricks, woodwork and glass. Other tile arrangements are numerous

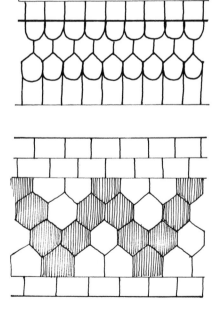

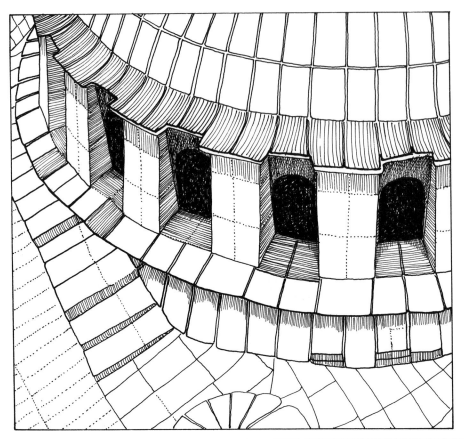

**81** The curving tile-pattern on the roof of a mosque

**82** Detail from 'Roofs of Florence' by Audrey Ormrod. The high ridges of the tiles have been achieved in various ways—raised chain band, padded leather, rolls and pleats of felt, knitting, needleweaving, beads, satin stitch over padding, chain and straight stitches

**83** Undulating and overlapping sections of tiles resemble Italian quilting over cutwork windows. (*Photo : V. A. Campbell-Harding*)

**84** As an exercise, translate this pattern of tiles into embroidery, trying to imitate the diagonal ridges of the lines, and also the horizontal ones which break up towards the top

**85** Various patterns made by tiles, brick and stonework

**86** Tiles and stonework in France. (*Photo: V. A. Campbell-Harding*)

**87** A close-up of the patterns and textures of tiles overhanging a rough stone wall, with the gutter between, allowing shafts of light to penetrate from above. (*Photo: V. A. Campbell-Harding*)

**88a** Scaffolding creates a network pattern of stitchery

**88b** A design based on patterns of scaffolding by Christine Evans. Over a background of patterned fabric, pieces of silk and lines of machine stitching suggest the criss-crossing of metal framework. (*Photo: Christine Evans*)

**89** A canvaswork exercise by Jennie Parry, with ribbons, beads and pailettes, gold purl and metal threads. The stitches, especially those in the upper part of the sample, have the quality of pattern seen in the scaffolding in fig. 88a. (*Photo: V. A. Campbell-Harding*)

**90** Flats and scaffolding at the Barbican Centre, London

**91** A drawing made from a newspaper photograph of workmen in silhouette, returning to their work at the top of a building site

58

# Doors and Arches

Doors have a special significance to many people. Closed doors seem to imply that progress in a certain direction is halted, perhaps only temporarily, perhaps permanently. It implies a time for re-assessment, decisions, redirection. Open doors seem to be an invitation to proceed, to investigate, especially those which are wide open where the view beyond is clearly visible and therefore holds little fear of the unknown. Doors which are slightly ajar, however, imply more caution in progress especially if the colour-tone seen beyond the door is darker than the rest. If we approach a door through which light streams towards us we are drawn nearer in an automatic gesture of release, freedom and perhaps safety.

Doors and gateways are so varied in style and decoration that one could easily work on this subject alone for a long time without repeating an idea. They make interesting motifs for experimental work because of their basically simple shapes, and the more elaborate ones may be the basis of larger projects in mixed techniques. Placed on small pockets, bags and purses they make ideal decorations, giving added meaning to the function of the articles. The geometric nature of the subject also makes it ideal for counted-thread embroidery, which includes canvaswork, pulled work, drawn thread work, cross stitch and blackwork.

It is more often in large buildings, old and new, that the structure of rafters and beams is apparent, as they form both functional and decorative elements in public architecture.

Look upwards and see the mass of beams and supports above your head; notice the patterns, shapes and spaces between the lines. Don't be overawed by perspective but see it in terms of pattern and abstract design. Drawing constructions such as these may be a problem unless the observer is well-practised, so it is often easier to take a photograph or to use one seen in a book. It may be simplified to make the pattern less complex, to accentuate the solid or lacey effects or to make it more suitable for a particular embroidery technique.

Arcades and arches fulfil similar purposes in design by concentrating the eye towards a certain point inside the arch, or to a point in the distance framed by arches, whilst repeated arches form patterns which may be used out of context. Sometimes the structure itself is more interesting than the shapes contained inside it and at other times, the shape inside, and its decoration, is all-important.

For design purposes, don't be intimidated by the different styles which have evolved throughout the centuries; you can mix them together quite successfully if you wish, without knowing their origins, although the more complex Islamic styles certainly have a unique flavour.

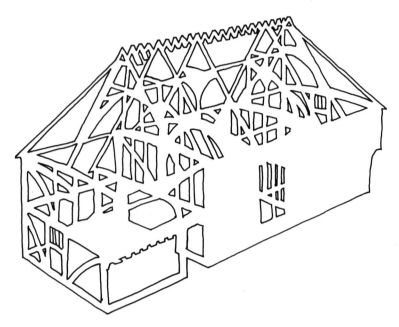

**92** A drawing of a framework construction of the fourteenth century, showing how only the areas of light have been outlined and all other details have been omitted

**93** Timber beams of a collar-braced roof of the fourteenth century create a solid and well-balanced pattern of diagonal lines filled with contrasting curves. No light and shade is shown here, in an attempt to abstract the shapes from their actual function. Even more simplification could be attempted to achieve this effect

**94** Iron beams supporting the glass roof of Victoria Coach Station in London. To simplify this lace-like effect, capture a small part in a window of plain paper

**95** A richly-coloured stained-glass window accentuates the semi-circular end of this shopping arcade in Norwich, echoing the beams above and the windows at the sides. Rectangular shapes are seen in both sets of windows, and in the brickwork

**96a**

**96** Old wooden beams of an ancient tithe-barn shown in two different interpretations, producing images of night and day. Figure 96a suggests cutwork embroidery while Figure 96b would make an interesting design using appliqué, shadow-quilting or English quilting

**96b**

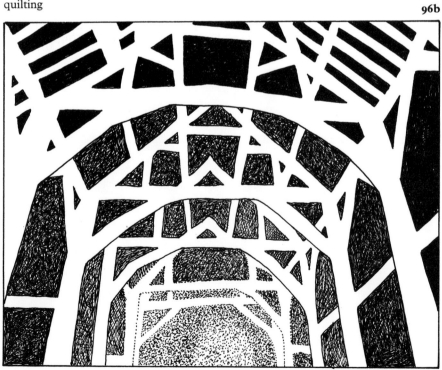

97

98

**97, 98** Outdoor and indoor corridors, both leading the eye positively to the square exit in the centre by means of vertical, horizontal and diagonal lines. The upright rectangular areas seen at the sides between supports are interesting for different reasons in both pictures. In Figure 97 the garden area actually frames the central focal point

**99** Curved arches may be seen to better advantage when enclosed within a circular frame. Omit details which are not essential to the design, and do not feel obliged to place the focal point in the dead centre of the shape. Nevertheless, the focal point (which is the door in this case) must be a comfortable distance inside the circle, in order to maintain its importance. This distance can be determined by moving the circular paper window over the picture until a balance is found between the larger dark and the smaller light areas.

**100** A five-sided mesh screen embroidered by Jennie Parry. (*Photo : Jennie Parry*)

**101** The Islamic arches of a mosque at Karouhan, Tunisia. For design purposes, perspective may be ignored and the main shapes drawn as though directly from the front. (*Photo : Susan Messent*)

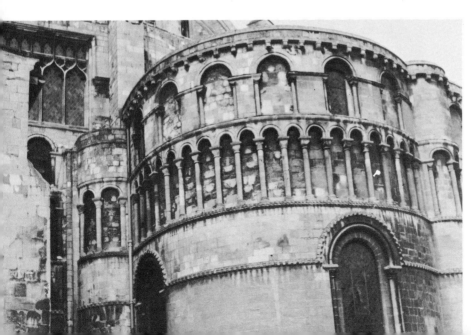

**102** Decorative arches on Norwich Cathedral

103 ABOVE LEFT Decoration on a huge Gothic door showing beautifully patterned arches of different sizes. (*Victoria and Albert Museum, London*)

104 ABOVE A rustic stone archway blends with the landscape, and the texture of the stone contrasts with the foliage

105 A pattern of curved and straight lines, dark and lighter tones, hard and soft textures, makes an interesting design. (*Photo: V. A. Campbell-Harding*)

**106** Another fascinating arrangement of straight and curved lines and shapes, patterned and plain areas and tonal variations. Through almost closed eyes you will be able to see the four main tonal areas. (*Photo: V. A. Campbell-Harding*)

**107** The foliage seen in this indoor corridor softens the formal aspect of the straight lines

**108** BELOW LEFT A view into a private room makes an interesting subject which may be interpreted by means of an uncoloured door and frame (plain calico perhaps?) and a coloured interior

**109** A view from inside looking outwards to a topiary garden. The pattern of stonework and stairs makes an unusual frame for the central area of light

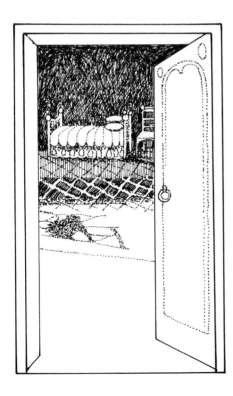

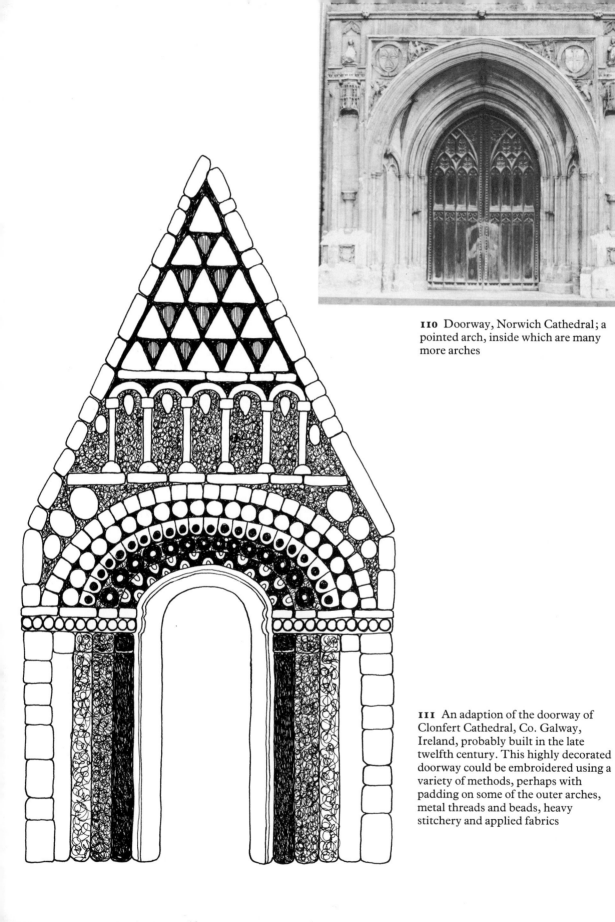

**110** Doorway, Norwich Cathedral; a pointed arch, inside which are many more arches

**111** An adaption of the doorway of Clonfert Cathedral, Co. Galway, Ireland, probably built in the late twelfth century. This highly decorated doorway could be embroidered using a variety of methods, perhaps with padding on some of the outer arches, metal threads and beads, heavy stitchery and applied fabrics

112 Carved stonework forming long ridges (perhaps Italian quilting or heavy cords?) and overlapping arches. The heavy doors show a bold scroll pattern of ironwork

113 Another arched doorway with an interesting shape made by the richly-wrought iron gates and the overhead decoration

114, 115 Two versions of the well-known doorway of Kilpeck Church in Herefordshire, embroidered by Jan Attrill. One shows metal thread work and padding, the other shows stonework of quilting on painted fabric

116 Felt appliqué and machine embroidery in an experiment by Jennie Parry. (*Photo : V. A. Campbell-Harding*)

117 A heavy, ornamental doorway of plasterwork makes an imposing entrance to an eighteenth-century house

118 RIGHT An ancient door frame surrounds this simple door in Norwich

119 BELOW Richly-textured and patterned stonework makes a perfect design for embroidery. Notice also the bearded head over the doorway, and the shape of the glass in the windows on the right

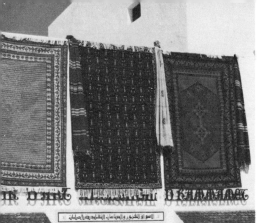

**120** Oriental carpets decorate the front of this bazaar in Tunisia with its decorated doorway. Note also the decoration on the open door inside the arch, and the iron railing in the foreground. (*Photo : Susan Messent*)

**121** Decorative brickwork and carved timber make a design rich with pattern. The door-within-a-door is a feature of very old houses. (*Photo : V. A. Campbell-Harding*)

**122** Four doors, the smallest showing
another door within

1 'Cognac Martell, Normandy Farmhouse,'
by Barbara Seidlecka. A panel measuring
approximately 122 x 91 cm (48 x 36 in.),
embroidered on a background of sprayed blanket
material, with yarns ranging from string to silk.
*(Photo: Barbara Seidlecka)*

**2** 'Platform 3, Victoria Station,' by Barbara Seidlecka.
A panel measuring 76 x 76 cm (30 x 30 in.) showing
a view from platform 3 on a misty November day.
The view now no longer exists. Old fabrics are
embroidered with a variety of yarns, and chalk,
charcoal, ink and graphite are used to create a rather
worn-out look. *(Photo: Barbara Seidlecka)*

**123** Wrought iron decoration inset on a wooden frame

**124** Wrought iron surrounding the Albert Memorial, London. Compare one of these design elements to those in fig. 120. As seen in Fig. 125, the elements may be isolated, simplified and used in a different arrangement

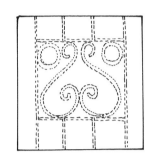

**125** Simplified elements can be translated into patterns suitable for quilting. These are particularly useful for garments and accessories. The ironwork pattern on the door would also look well embroidered onto a jacket or waistcoat, and the door handle pattern on a pocket or bag. Even the keyhole is decorated!

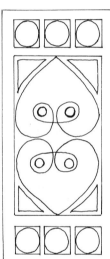

**126** Delicate gates show up against the white house beyond, and contrast with the heavy foliage above. Sonning, Berkshire

**128** A gateway designed by Antoni Gaudí showing an unusual patchwork-type arrangement where the shapes inside the lines appear more important than the lines themselves.

**130** A gateway at Lindisfarne; the heavy and solid stonework in the foreground is repeated on the building in the distance. (*Photo: V. A. Campbell-Harding*)

**127** A garden gate of wrought iron. Notice the extra pattern made inside a square by four of the centre 'knobs'

**129** Another patchwork-type design achieved by the geometric nature of the gates and the paler building beyond them. Looked at through half-closed eyes this becomes almost abstract

# Windows

The significance of windows in our minds is similar to that of doors: we can see them from both inside and outside, open and closed, inviting or secretive, revealing or reflecting, sometimes both. Quite apart from the decorative aspect of windows and window-frames, this special significance might be investigated in more depth by the embroiderer to lead eventually to a series of works based on one's own progress through life, or perhaps depicting, in symbolic terms, a sequence of events. Barred windows denote imprisonment, open ones imply freedom, half-drawn curtains may suggest a request for privacy, while no curtains at all (especially at large windows) may create a feeling of exposure and vulnerability, although this would also depend to some extent on the view outside. These basic concepts may mean different things to different people; it is by no means always necessary to attach a hidden meaning to a design, though sometimes this can be fun.

The bonus which this subject has as a design source is, of course, the glass. Apart from our ability to see both inside and outside at the same time, and also through to the other side of the building, we can even see what is behind us reflected in windows (fig. 146). Glass is also coloured in many different styles; the modern approach to stained glass is quite different from that of earlier artists, and small areas of stained glass with the sun shining through make pools of colour flooding over objects in its path. Small panes of glass are made in many shapes and arranged in patterns some of which are identical to blackwork stitches and to certain patchwork arrangements.

**131** These three shop-fronts may be embroidered separately or placed side-by-side in a long row. Other shops in a series like this might include a chemist, butcher, antique shop, book shop, draper/haberdasher, milliner, grocer and greengrocer

**132** An elegant set of windows in an old building in Norwich. The door-window echoes the same pattern, with the addition of an extra set of lower panes. Imagine the window-boxes in full bloom, and create a design based on these units

**133** A large bay window at Hampton Court Palace, topped by patterned stonework and surrounded by old red brickwork

**134** A long window on a timber and brickwork building which would adapt well to various techniques, including patchwork, canvaswork, free stitchery or quilting

**135** The ingenuity of builders is evident in the variety of window shapes, the surrounding frames of stone, wood or brickwork, the shape of the glass panes and the arrangement of the various parts to make a complete unit. These examples may be added to imaginary building designs, or worked alone. A large design could be made to have panes of glass which open (i.e. in three dimensions) to reveal a scene inside

**136** Ancient churches and cathedrals often have large, round windows known as rose windows inset with delicately carved stonework resembling lace mats. This one, photographed by Margaret Hake, was the basis of a design for a set of table mats

**137** Table mats, designed and made by Margaret Hake. The smaller mat uses only the central part of the window pattern

**138** Designs adapted from the rose windows of several European cathedrals, including Chartres, Notre Dame, Bourges and Lincoln. These beautiful motifs may be used as decorations on dress and accessories, for stool and table-tops, box-tops, table linen and cushions. They would also be particularly relevant on ecclesiastical garments and linen, in goldwork or in monochrome embroidery

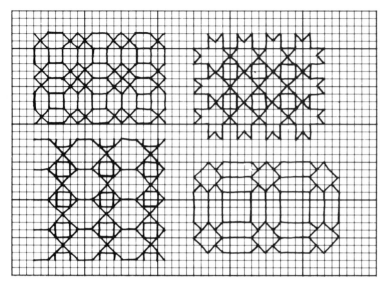

**139** Church windows are often good sources of blackwork patterns. The ones shown here are all taken from churches

**140** A fascinating pattern of reflections seen in a church window, and also a clear view of windows on the other side of the building

**141** Another blackwork pattern seen in small panes of glass creating an over-all lacey effect over what looks like crumpled transparent paper

**142** Windows in the Art Nouveau style are instantly recognizable by their flowing curves, rounded corners and bold patchwork shapes. The three rounded windows are by Antoni Gaudí. The smaller rectangular window showing a knight at prayer is much older and illustrates a more haphazard mixture of shapes and pattern

**143** Stained glass patterns are ideal for patchwork, counted thread work and cutwork. Top left: American (detail), top right: English (detail), bottom left: French

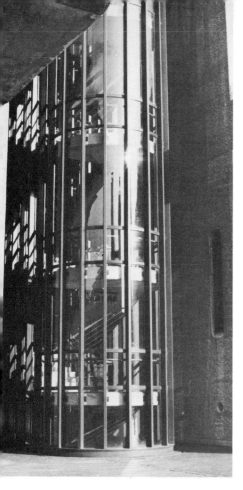

**144** ABOVE Reflections of tower blocks seen in the conservatory window at the Barbican Centre. A small area could be taken from this photograph to form the basis of a design

**145** LEFT A tall cylindrical window at the Barbican Centre, London

**146** Buildings on three vertical planes: the inside of the office block on the right, the buildings on the other side of it, and those behind the viewer which are reflected in the glass on the left. This overlapping of features is a design point easily simulated in embroidery by the use of transparent fabrics

**147** An effect similar to that in figure 146 is seen in this three-plane photograph of the Albert Hall foyer in London

**148** Modern tower blocks often incorporate extensive areas of glass, sometimes smokey-brown, sometimes like huge bronze mirrors designed to reflect the textures opposite. This huge set of windows in London reflects rippling lines, giving expression to what would otherwise be a blank stare. (*Photo : V. A. Campbell-Harding*)

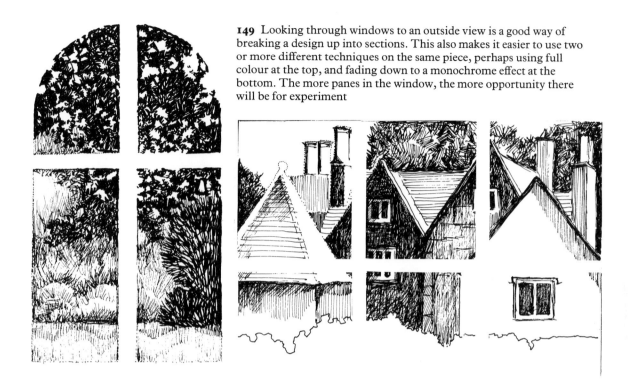

**149** Looking through windows to an outside view is a good way of breaking a design up into sections. This also makes it easier to use two or more different techniques on the same piece, perhaps using full colour at the top, and fading down to a monochrome effect at the bottom. The more panes in the window, the more opportunity there will be for experiment

**150** A cottage window surrounded by rough brickwork and tall summer flowers. Note the decorative arrangement of bricks surrounding the window frame

# Stairs and Steps

Many of the best outdoor examples of steps have to be discovered by inquisitive embroiderers who have no qualms about prying into quiet courtyards, or peeping through archways and into back-alleys. Fire-escapes are almost always tucked away in a hidden spot but are decorative seen from any angle, especially underneath.

Photographs of steps and stairs are particularly useful, as perspective can be a problem: a photograph will clearly show the relationship of the various sections—treads, risers and banisters or rails.

The formal arrangement of lines, the spaces and the balance of the structure as a whole are very satisfying to a designer looking for similar patterns and effects. The very materials from which steps and stairs are made convey completely different images to us: wrought iron and wood at railway stations, metal stairs outside buildings, brick ones blending into modern shopping precincts and polished wooden ones with carved banisters turn to right and left with dignity in great houses.

Spiral staircases have an individual and unique quality. For one thing, they are very rarely (if ever) made to accommodate more than one person on the same tread, one cannot usually see one's point of destination from either top or bottom (which generates an element of surprise on arrival!), and they are so reminiscent of ancient stone castles, windmills and lighthouses that, in my imagination, they create a feeling of unreality and secretiveness. My own fascination for them will be revealed by the fact that I have illustrated several in this book.

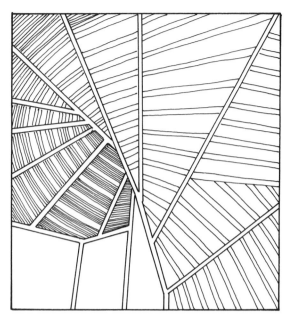

**151** The underside of a wooden spiral staircase clearly shows the decorative arrangement of supports

**152** Looking upwards to the inside of a church spire built by Antoni Gaudi, showing the light beaming down onto the various levels

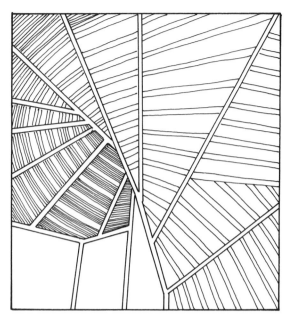

**154** The underside of a stone spiral staircase by Gaudi, resembling a snail's shell

**153** A grand spiral staircase in a stately home with wrought-iron balustrades giving an impression of light and delicacy

**155** Drawn from an advertisement photograph, this design is equally balanced when turned upside down or sideways

**156** The fire escape at Grantley Hall, Yorkshire. The central post from which all the steps spring is clearly seen, and each curve from door to door is identical

**157** Another fire escape zigzags between two outside walls, lending even more decoration to an already richly decorated building

**158** A zigzag pattern of stone steps, with delicate ironwork, railings and foliage

**159** Brick steps in Reading, Berkshire, contrast with the roughness of the older building beyond. This bricked pavement area is tucked away between new and old buildings where the general public rarely goes

**160** Walk slowly up outdoor steps to take in the view of lines appearing at your sides over the top step. Note all the lines in this photograph, including those made by the bricks of the steps, which appear as continuous lines at the right and as broken ones at the left

**161** Indoor stairs in modern buildings are often surrounded by glass panels to create an impression of space and light. This means that much of the structure which would normally be hidden from view is clearly seen at all levels, the glass reflecting lights and colours. Part of this photograph could be isolated within a 'window' of paper to block out the parts not required

**162** This drawing is almost abstract as all detail has been eliminated to reveal only the basic structure. It also looks interesting when turned upside-down. It was drawn from a photograph taken inside Manchester University

# Decoration

This particular aspect of architecture contains such a wealth of material that one could easily fill a book entirely with ideas based on the decorative features as distinct from the purely functional ones. Much of the time the two elements are interconnected, as functional structures are often formed in a decorative manner, such as the geometrical timber patterns on old houses in England. But compare these happy accidents to the truly purposeful attempts at beautification by some architects of modern multi-storey car-parks with intricately patterned concrete grills concealing their contents (fig. 174). Other decorations may be found as parts of doors and windows, and these (in their entirety) have been dealt with in their respective sections.

Sometimes, however, decoration on buildings was used solely as an outlet for man's creative urges, positively bubbling over in the Victorian era when no space was left empty, more sinuously curvaceous in the Art Nouveau period in the early 1900s, then even more restrained throughout the war years, the amount and style of decoration reflecting quite accurately the national priorities, affluence and aspirations. This is true not only of England, but even more so of the United States, where widely scattered communities developed and kept their own styles of decoration. Countries in which little has happened to change the way of life and where there have been no outside influences have not felt the same compulsion to change their style of decoration, though even now the paraphernalia of modern living can be detected on the outside walls of some African houses in the form of moulded plaster bicycles among the more traditional patterns.

Modern buildings often show restrained and cleverly devised decoration which sometimes gives an indication of its purpose. This concept is in total opposition to that of some much older buildings whose architects seemed intent on disguising the real function at all costs. Ingenious ways of using modern building materials in a decorative manner have led to different kinds of designs being initiated which reflect not only the spirit of the age but also the inventiveness (and sometimes the sheer brilliance) of man.

As embroiderers searching for ideas, take time to look about you— around corners, under arches, over barriers. Little decorative touches are

**163** The Albert Memorial, London. Every part of this monument is a source of design: the gables, the pinnacles, and the many figures which cover and surround it

often obscurely placed, waiting for you to notice them, even way above your head where the pigeons are perching.

**164** A Tudor building rich in decoration drawn in a way which outlines the patterns, any of which may be isolated and used out of context, or perhaps worked in English quilting or shadow quilting

**165** Timber patterns on old houses at Chartres, France

**166** Houses at Lavenham, Suffolk, show decorative wood carving around the door, windows and corner-posts, as well as patterned wood-framing. (*Photo: V. A. Campbell-Harding*)

3 'Living City' by Barbara Seidlecka. A large panel, designed so that the lower dark part fades into a dark wall and light catches the lighter yarns and metal threads; the tonal emphasis changes throughout the day with the changing light, as happens in a living city. *(By courtesy of Credit Suisse Bank. Photo: Barbara Seidlecka)*

4 Skeleton of a wooden barn in Hampshire: a mass of parallel lines and angles, some criss-crossing others as threads do. The trees beyond and the dried grasses in the foreground might be translated into masses of straight stitches while the more solid lines of the ruin could be expressed as blackwork, appliqué, couching or simply heavier lines of stitches such as chain and raised chain band. *(Photo: Jan Messent)*

**5** Detail of 'Radcliffe Library, Oxford' by Roy Hirst. The complete embroidery is shown in the chapter on Spires, Towers and Domes. *(Photo: Roy Hirst)*

**6** Shuttered windows and doors in a French village: simple related shapes call for a simple treatment, whilst rich textural effects may be used on the foliage and railings. *(Photo: V. A. Campbell-Harding)*

**167** The side view of a timber-framed
house on a raised stone base

**168** The back of a large timber-framed
manor house with clusters of ornamental
chimneys and a very large diamond-paned
window

**169** Barge-boards are carved wooden decorations attached to the gable end of some houses. These examples were all taken from British Railway station buildings

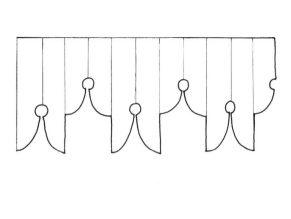

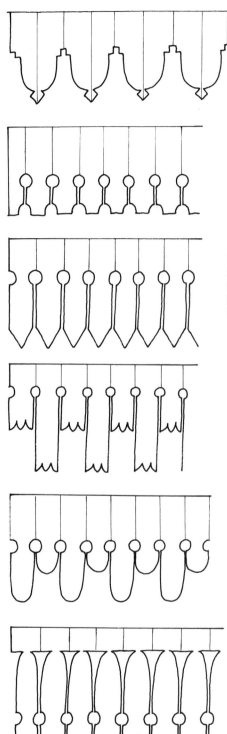

**170** Railway stations were often decorated with valances made from wooden planks, each railway company having its own kind of design. The arrangement of the planks to form a pattern is most ingenious and could be copied using strips of fabric to make patchwork

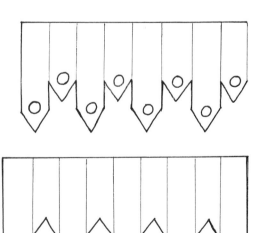

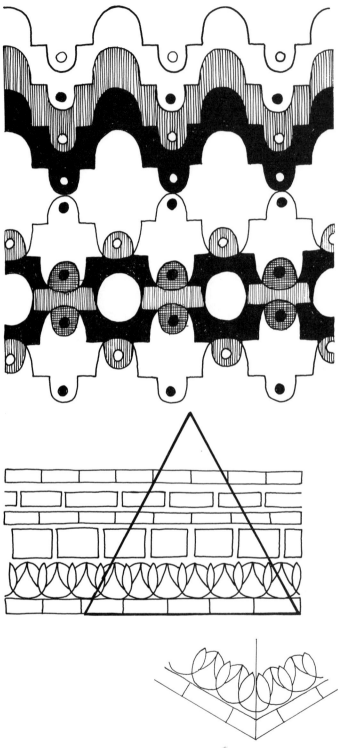

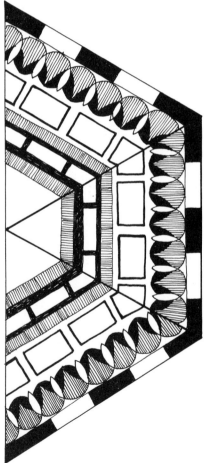

**171, 172** Ideas borrowed from
Jennie Parry's notebook. Designs
based on a barge-board (top), and a
Victorian brickwork pattern
(bottom). In the lower design, the
problem of the corners may be
resolved by slightly re-arranging the
shapes inside the units as shown in
the small corner diagram

**173** A photograph of wooden blocks formerly used in the printing of fabrics, now nailed to the end of a barn in Oxfordshire. This could be envisaged as adjoining rectangles of canvas embroidery or goldwork. (*Photo : V. A. Campbell-Harding*)

**174** The concrete moulded slabs used to disguise a multi-storey car-park in Reading, Berkshire. The joins between the sections can clearly be seen, and each horizontal row of sections is repeated

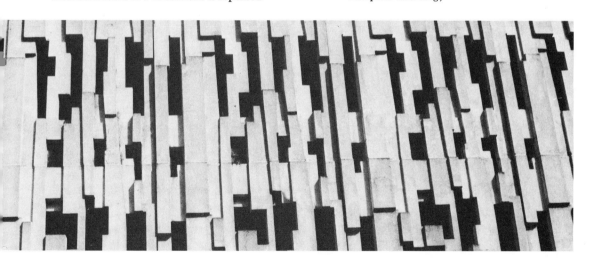

**175** Smaller concrete units on a wall show two different textures. The units are not identical

**176, 177** This ingenious wall-decoration consists of two design units used in a variety of different positions, as seen in the upper diagram. It is part of the Manchester University buildings. The two separate units are seen on the left of the drawing

**178** Sculpture on the outside wall of an insurance building in Reading, Berkshire, suggesting textile fabrics such as pleated calico, wrapped cords and Italian quilting

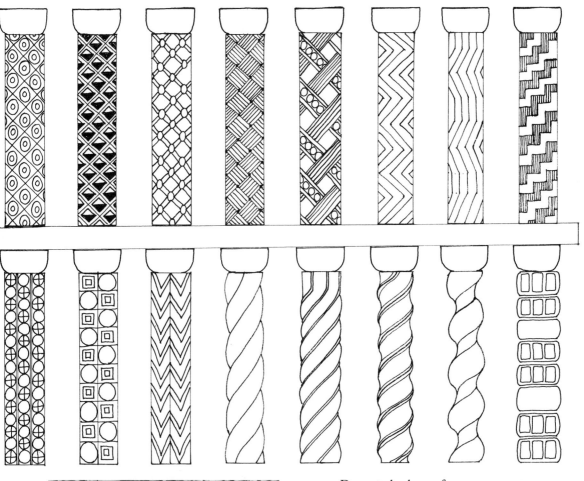

**179** Decorated columns from many sources

**180** Part of the vaulting and ceiling decoration under the main archway of Hampton Court Palace, Kingston-upon-Thames

**181** Tile and stone patterns from Islamic buildings. These are usually geometric in nature, and are good sources of border patterns and motifs. The border seen at the top is a repeating pattern which begins again at the extreme right

**182** Islamic wood-carving, with gold paint and inlaid mother-of-pearl. This is basically a simple geometric design which could be translated into quilting or canvaswork

**183, 184** Celtic strapwork motifs can be made more complex by splitting the interlacing band into two, and making both strands weave separately. Bottom right: French (adapted); top right: French; bottom left: Early eleventh-century Polish Romanesque

**185** A Celtic motif carved in stone at the base of a larger cross.

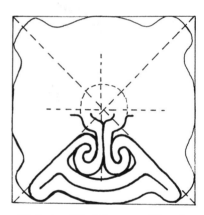

**186** A simplified diagram of fig. 185

**187** Celtic interlaced design. This complex motif appears to consist of two pairs of men, each of whose arms (and legs?) are interwoven to grasp each other's hair. Their beards (or tongues?) develop into twisted coils which fill in the gaps

**188** Saxon and Celtic crosses. The larger, more detailed cross is of Viking origin from Middleton in Yorkshire, showing a warrior in his grave

**189** An ancient Saxon device of squared spirals carved above a doorway. This is part of a repeating border pattern

**190** The carved stone decoration from a doorway in St Peter's Church, Britford, Wiltshire

**191** Two of the Queen's Beasts on their pedestals seen here at Hampton Court Palace, with a third one in the distance (bottom left-hand corner). They may also be seen at Kew Gardens near Richmond. The beautifully decorated chimneys are visible

**192** A deer and her fawn stand on the gate posts of Hyde Park in London. The bare trees provide an attractive background resembling needleweaving against padded leather

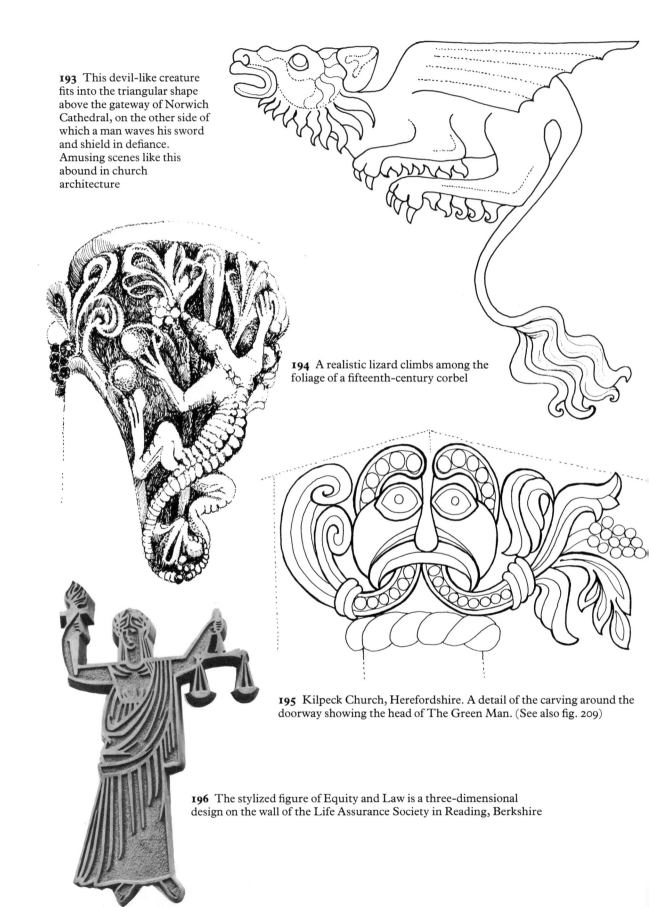

**193** This devil-like creature fits into the triangular shape above the gateway of Norwich Cathedral, on the other side of which a man waves his sword and shield in defiance. Amusing scenes like this abound in church architecture

**194** A realistic lizard climbs among the foliage of a fifteenth-century corbel

**195** Kilpeck Church, Herefordshire. A detail of the carving around the doorway showing the head of The Green Man. (See also fig. 209)

**196** The stylized figure of Equity and Law is a three-dimensional design on the wall of the Life Assurance Society in Reading, Berkshire

197 Two cavaliers are carved in relief from the stone blocks forming the side of the building at 76 Bury Street, London SW1

198 Three young figures contrast in texture and shape with the vertical and horizontal rigidity of the buildings surrounding them

199 A delightful sculpture, also in Reading, of a young man cartwheeling across a ledge of brickwork, his movement accentuated by the curving bricks behind him

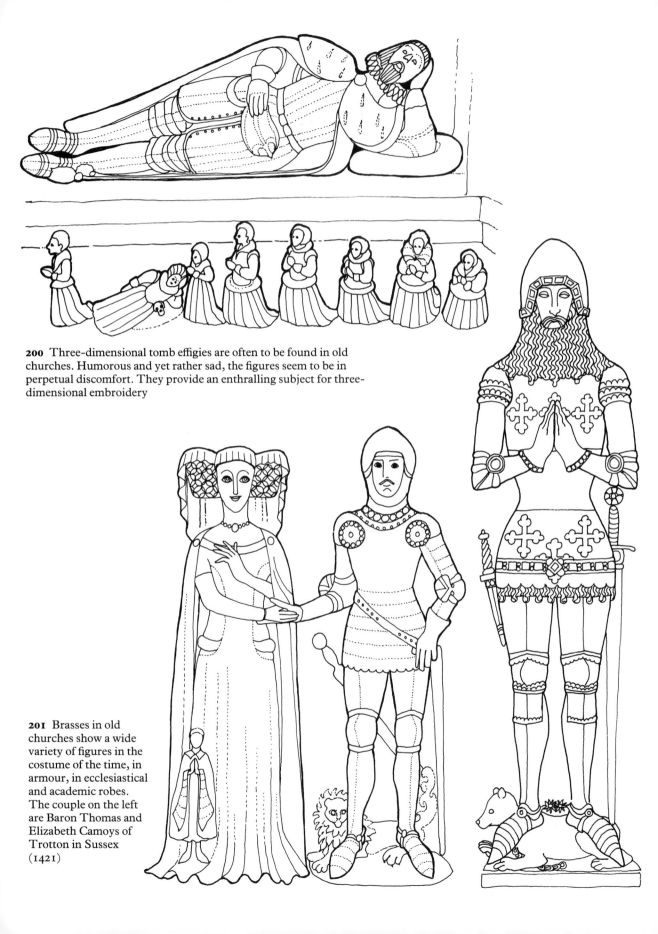

**200** Three-dimensional tomb effigies are often to be found in old churches. Humorous and yet rather sad, the figures seem to be in perpetual discomfort. They provide an enthralling subject for three-dimensional embroidery

**201** Brasses in old churches show a wide variety of figures in the costume of the time, in armour, in ecclesiastical and academic robes. The couple on the left are Baron Thomas and Elizabeth Camoys of Trotton in Sussex (1421)

**202** These beautifully stylized heads of carved stone are arranged in an arch around the doorway of Kilpeck Church in Herefordshire. There are many more to be seen on the same doorway.

**203** Three faces in one head; a stone corbel showing both profiles and full-face

**204** A lion's head cast-iron door-knocker. This could be effectively worked in coloured felts as a circular panel for a child's room

**205** Cast-iron door-knocker. (*Victoria and Albert Museum*)

**206, 207** Cast-iron door-knockers resembling the legendary Wild Men of the Woods of the German Middle Ages. (*Victoria and Albert Museum*)

**208** Two back-to-back figures hold up the same capital whilst being shackled hand and foot. The clearly-cut, flowing lines are perfect for embroidery in couching, goldwork and padding. From the portal of Oloron Ste Marie. French Romanesque

**209** The Green Man, one of many interpretations of the ancient legendary figure who is always shown with foliage issuing from his mouth. This one is in Old Radnor Church, Powys

**210** A carved marble mask; the mouth is a gaping hole. From the theatre, Ostia, Italy

**211** A detail from the portal above the doorway at St Genis des Fontaines (1019–1020) showing three of the apostles surrounding Christ. This type of design is especially suitable for goldwork, couching and quilting, but could also be much simplified for other techniques

**212, 213, 214, 215** Four decorative lamps of different designs

214

215

**216** 'The Sculpture for Lighting' hangs in the foyer of
the Barbican Centre, London. It was designed by the
Australian Michel J. Santry

# Spires, Towers and Domes

**217** Towers and turrets are an essential part of the fantastic building, for they epitomise romance, fairy tales and magic events. Fortunately there is no shortage of material from which to borrow shapes and ornament, for architects throughout the ages and in every country have made use of these decorative accessories

**218** Spires stress the importance of a building by making it higher than others around it. These additions will help to create a focal point, so they should be placed where the designer wishes the eye to explore longest and finally come to rest

**219** The Radcliffe Library, Oxford; an embroidery by Roy Hirst using straight machine stitches on a dye-painted background. (*Photo : Roy Hirst*)

**220** The thirteenth-century outer walls and towers at Carcassonne in France—a wealth of towers and turrets, arches and battlements (*Photo : V. A. Campbell-Harding*)

**221** The well-known and richly-ornamented onion
domes of the eleventh-century St Basil's Cathedral,
Moscow. These domes are arranged in a square
formation, and the design calls for a rich treatment of
applied fabrics, crusty stitchery and metal threads with
beads

**222, 223** Two patterns of eastern domes and minarets by Susan Messent. Use tracing paper for this kind of exercise, laying the outlines over each other to create interesting shapes where they overlap

**224** An embroidery by Vera Bradshaw of Islamic buildings, arches, towers and rich pattern. The foliage in the foreground is a perfect foil to the flat stitchery ornamentation, with small areas of felt and padded leather

**225** Chinese pagodas are highly decorative and may be seen in ornamental gardens all over the world. The main element is repeated many times, getting smaller towards the top. The rectangular elements of the tower in the centre are all different, but unity can be achieved in the choice of colours and stitches. The Anglo-Saxon tower on the right has a quilted appearance, but the strips could also be made of heavy cord or raised satin stitch

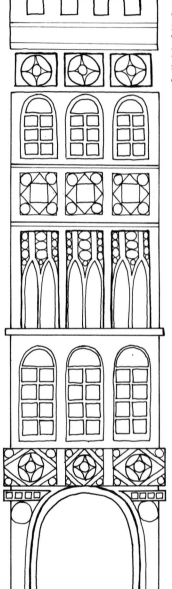

# Architecture in the Environment

Buildings blending into the landscape, clustering into a valley, lining the sea-front or straggling along a cobbled street can provide a focal point which may also be reached along a road or path, a line of walling or steps. The environment itself may be of either primary or secondary importance to the design, but the way in which buildings are grouped, scattered or isolated, and their position in relation to the edges of the 'picture' should be very carefully considered, as they will almost certainly be instrumental in attracting and holding the attention of the eye. A line of buildings running from one side across the design to the other side will probably need such extra details as window-boxes, foliage, people, etc., to arrest the attention and invite further exploration.

The following illustrations will suggest ways in which the medium of embroidery has an advantage over the more conventional illustrative techniques, as being an excellent *design* medium it can take liberties with texture, pattern and shape to make a subject much more than merely a picture.

As well as the more everyday buildings of houses and shops, consider also those which are just as decorative but often taken for granted: office-blocks, mills (especially old stone-built ones), oil rigs, lighthouses, gas-holders, pylons, water-coolers, etc. Although rows of stone-built Cotswold houses and thatched cottages may be an attractive subject, remember that a design need not rely on 'prettiness' to be valid; a carefully worked-out study of industrial architecture can be much more informative and interesting if tackled with an open mind and an eye which is able to observe beauty in power, and sometimes in ugliness itself.

**226** A row of town houses worked in canvas embroidery

**227** Houses with roofs of different shapes. A design such as this could easily be translated into appliqué and free stitchery, cross stitch or canvaswork

**228, 229** Two methods of presenting small sections of embroidery; both ideas may be added to at later stages with more strips or squares. The one on the right could perhaps be a record of the designer's homes

**230** Canvaswork combined with crochet loop stitch. Lower down, the doors are reflected in the stream. The stonework of the cottages was worked partly in a random-dyed knitting yarn to suggest the variations in colour

124

**231** Grantley Hall in North
Yorkshire seen from the
shadow of a huge cedar tree.
The intriguing glimpse of the
stone house in the distance
may suggest delicate stitchery
against heavily padded trees in
the foreground

**232** The opposite is the case
in this drawing of an American
verandah cottage where the
foreground is left untreated,
all attention being focused on
the building and foliage
beyond the fence

**233** Farm buildings and oast-houses provide an assortment of roof shapes, angles and textures

**234** A solitary windmill on the horizon evokes a feeling of wind and sky and wide open spaces. A heavy sky of dark clouds would increase this feeling to one of threat and exposure. The patterns of the hay in the field not only lead the eye towards the focal point but also suggest the undulations of the ground

**235** A lighthouse seen against a stylized sky of windswept clouds. This interpretation suggests a quilted and padded foreground with a minimum of detail, against a background of applied fabrics

**236** The lace-like structure of a gas-holder suggests machine embroidery, blackwork, couching, free stitchery or knitting

**237** Mills and power stations also have their place in design as this silhouette of Battersea Power Station shows. The wheeling gulls over the water in the foreground lend depth and scale to the design

**238** A drawing which could not be ignored even though the architecture is almost hidden. A background of 'scribbled' stitchery, machine embroidery or ragged applied fabric would express the sketchy appearance, leaving the washing void

239

240 Aerial views of buildings show up patterns un-noticed at ground level. These glass-houses create a pattern similar to applied strips of fabric, with realistic stitchery buildings and foliage between them

OPPOSITE BELOW

239 This is a subject with enormous scope for different embroidery techniques, suitable for both coloured and monochrome translations. It would also adapt well to the type of presentation shown in fig. 228

241 Lyn Hughes' embroidery of a Swiss meadow is worked in assorted threads and stitches on calico dyed with 'fun' dyes; a delightful holiday record in embroidery

**242** Eastbourne pier. The fanciful pavilions and lacework supports make seaside piers an extremely decorative subject for embroidery. (*Photo: R. Keith Messent*)

**243** A sensitive drawing by Sarah Harding of roof-tops blurred into each other like patches of textured fabric or stitchery. (*Photo: V. A. Campbell-Harding*)

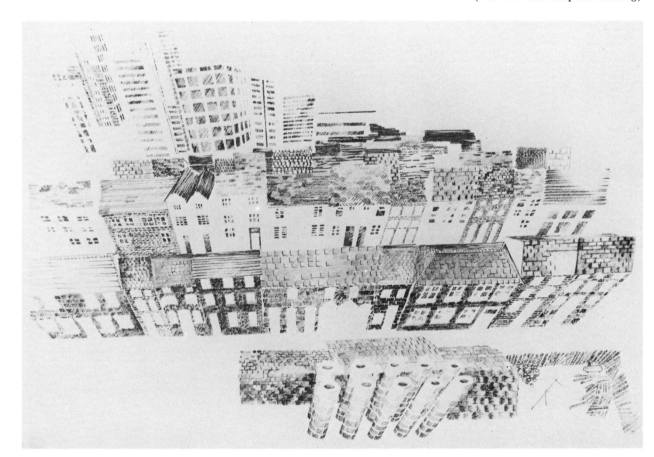

244 ABOVE LEFT Modern ironwork bridges symbolize power and strength with their heavy girders and brickwork, even though some are suspended delicately over water in a slim curve. This almost abstract design shows only a small section of a double bridge meant for both railway and cars

245 ABOVE A much simplified drawing of part of the Great Wall of China

246 The ancient city wall at York leads the eye towards the Minster in the distance

**247** The bridge at Sonning, Berkshire; a mixture of textures in the smooth water and tree-trunks, the brickwork and the foliage. A suggestion of a reflection is seen in the water

**248** A simplified drawing of another old bridge, excluding all textures but concentrating on shapes and lines only

**249** Houses and water at Norwich. The pattern of roof-tiles and the shapes of the buildings are particularly attractive

**250** Wood and water make an interesting pattern of diagonal and vertical lines

**251** Dripping water over mossy stones into a still pool suggests all kinds of fabric and yarn textures, perhaps with metal threads and beads for the water, and padded velvets and knitting for the boulders

# Ruins

The appeal of ruined architecture probably lies for most people in its evocation of time and history: a feeling of having been left behind, now out-of-place, unused and un-needed. Ruins stand out of time, regarding the modern world in their raiments of hand-made finery, now ragged and torn but often still magnificent, sometimes accentuating the quality of their materials by the fact that they are left standing while modern, cheaper versions are already forgotten rubble. Precious ruins with a dramatic past, like those at Coventry, are lovingly enclosed within newer and protective precincts, and some are guarded jealously against man's destruction although they have already stood against the elements for thousands of years. Every kind of ruin, whether ancient or merely old, has its own appeal and attraction for some reason, perhaps because it offers a designer a less rigid format than a complete building, with a more crumbled outline and more texture than shape. Delicate ornamentation seems even more delicate when it adjoins roughly ruined masonry, posing a challenge to the embroiderer which may suggest a series of experiments in several techniques.

Demolition sites are sad and dirty places, but may reveal interesting aspects of this theme such as interior colour and ornamentation, outlines of stairs and chimneys on inside walls and other out-of-context features which hang suspended before being removed from the public gaze.

252 Abbey ruins, taken from a photograph by V. A. Campbell-Harding; the strong shadows eliminate much of the detail to form a design of strong tones suitable for blackwork, or any other technique which relies on tonal and textural effects rather than colour

**253** Collapsed roof-tiles in France. (*Photo : V. A. Campbell-Harding*)

**254** Textural contrasts are seen here in the smoothness of the lawns, path and archway, and the rough stone and rubble walls. This could be accentuated in embroidery by padding and heavy 'crusty' stitchery

**255** Pattern and texture can clearly be seen in this photograph of a ruined abbey. The ridges on the lower wall suggest padded or quilted textured fabric. (*Photo : V. A. Campbell-Harding*)

257

**256** The arched shape of the frame is in keeping with the building seen mistily in the distance

**257** ABOVE RIGHT Depth is suggested by making darker the parts of the building which are nearest

**258** Brick and stonework ruins in France. (*Photo: V. A. Campbell-Harding*)

259 An Indian pueblo nestles under heavy overhanging cliffs in an almost futuristic scene of desolation. This scene offers many possibilities, either for tonal effects alone with many changes of texture, with paint and dyes sprayed under stitchery, or with machine embroidery and/or appliqué

260 'Lundy Cottages' by Barbara Seidlecka; Free machine quilting on calico, with crayon, ink, applied suede, string and velvet. (*Photo : Barbara Seidlecka*)

# Nature Takes Over

It takes almost as much effort on man's part to keep nature in its place as it does for him to erect a building. In spite of every effort to coax plants into good behaviour their appetites overcome even the greatest architectural feats eventually, as happened to the Mayan temples of the South American jungle and to the Inca mountain dwellings of Machu Pichu in Peru. There are countless instances where complete towns and villages (not to mention the island of Atlantis) have been lost to nature, some being engulfed by sea, lake and river, others by sand, volcanic ash and the debris of time.

The combination of architecture and nature is a useful one to designers, softening the edges of what might otherwise be too-rigid designs, hiding features which we find difficult to deal with, and adding colour and texture where this is needed.

Our subject has now come full circle: we are back at the beginning again with ground plans as the only indication of man's efforts in architecture (figs 51 and 52). Nature has indeed taken over, as it always does.

**261** Dried-out creepers cling for mutual protection to the rubble wall of a ruin in Norwich. This idea could be translated successfully in needleweaving over quilting, especially if the stonework was first patch-dyed to simulate the soft, changing colours

262 Rock plants lend a softer texture to a dry-stone garden wall, suggesting machine-stitched areas, pads of velvets, knitting and crochet and wrapped threads

263 The blossoms of early summer hang over an old red brick wall at Hampton Court Palace

264 The smooth, regular grey stone blocks are an excellent foil to this linear design of twisted branches

265 A gateway to the Forbury Gardens in Reading, Berkshire, with the old stone fountain in the distance. Foliage meets above the gates to form a canopy overhead, making a frame with the brickwork around the view of sunlit gardens

140

**266** Part of the hanging gardens in the conservatory of the Barbican Centre, London. The contrast of textures is even more accentuated here because of the smooth newness of the concrete balconies, their edges softened by the plants which pour over them.

**267** A drawing adapted from a photograph by V. A. Campbell-Harding. The background beyond the new concrete wall has been left out so that only three tones (including white and black) are seen. Make several tracings of this drawing, then re-arrange the three tones in various ways in each one to obtain different effects and emphasis

# Bibliography

## History of Embroidery

Bridgeman, Harriet and Drury, Elizabeth (editors), *Needlework, an Illustrated History*, Paddington Press 1978

King, Donald, *Samplers*, for the Victoria and Albert Museum by H.M.S.O. 1961

Lubell, Cecil (editor), *Textile Collections of the World Vols. I & II*, Studio Vista 1976

Wardle, Patricia, *Guide to English Embroidery*, for the Victoria and Albert Museum by H.M.S.O. 1970

## General Embroidery

Howard, Constance, *Inspiration for Embroidery*, Batsford 1968, reprinted 1985

Pyman, Kit (editor), *Needlecraft Series, Nos 1–16*, Search Press 1979–82

Whyte, Kathleen, *Design in Embroidery*, Batsford 1983

## Architecture

Automobile Association books: *The Book of British Towns; The Book of British Villages; The Past All Around Us; Treasures of Britain*

Adamson, Simon H., *Seaside Piers*, Batsford 1977

Anderson, V. R. and Fox, G. K., *A Pictorial Record of L.M.S. Architecture*, Oxford Publishing Co. 1981

Betjeman, John, *A Pictorial History of English Architecture*, Rainbird 1962

Brunskill, R. W., *The Illustrated Book of Vernacular Architecture*, Faber 1978

Burckhardt, Titus, *Art of Islam*, World of Islam Festival Publishing Co. 1976

Clifton-Taylor, Alec, *The Cathedrals of England*, Thames and Hudson 1976

Harbison, P., Potterton, H., and Sheehy, J., *Irish Art and Architecture*, Thames and Hudson 1978

Jellicoe, G. and S., *The Landscape of Man*, Thames and Hudson 1975

*Larousse Encyclopaedia of Byzantine and Medieval Art*, Paul Hamlyn 1963

Pevsner, Nikolaus, *The Sources of Modern Architecture and Design*, Thames and Hudson 1968

Prizeman, John, *Your House: The Outside View*, Hutchinson 1975

Reid, Richard, *The Book of Buildings. A Traveller's Guide*, Michael Joseph 1980

Smith, Cook and Hutton, *English Parish Churches*, Thames and Hudson 1976

Watkin, David, *A Concise History of English Architecture*, Thames and Hudson 1979

Yarwood, Doreen, *The Architecture of Britain*, Batsford 1976

Yarwood, Doreen, *The Architecture of Europe*, Batsford 1974

# Suppliers

**UK**
The Campden Needlecraft Centre, High Street, Chipping Campden, Gloucestershire
S. N. Cooke Ltd., 18 Wood Street, Stratford-on-Avon, Warwickshire
The Handicraft Shop, 5 Oxford Road, Altrincham, Cheshire
The Handworker's Market, 6 Bull Street, Holt, Norfolk NR25 6HP
Mace and Nairn, 89 Crane Street, Salisbury, Wiltshire SP1 2PY
Needle and Thread, 80 High Street, Horsell, Woking, Surrey
The Nimble Thimble, 26 The Green, Bilton, Rugby CV22 7LY
Richmond Art and Craft, Dept. E1, 181 City Road, Cardiff CF2 3JB
Christine Riley, 53 Barclay Street, Stonehaven, Kincardineshire AB3 2AR
Royal School of Needlework, 25 Princes Gate, London SW7 1QE
Spinning Jenny, Bradley, Keighley, West Yorkshire BD20 9DD
Teazle Embroideries, 35 Boothferry Road, Hull HU3 6UA

**USA**
Appleton Brothers of London, West Main Road, Little Compton, Rhode Island 02837
American Crewel Studio, Box 298, Boonton, New Jersey 07005
American Thread Corporation, 90 Park Avenue, New York
Bucky King Embroideries, Box 371, King Bros, 3 Ranch Buffalo Star Rte, Sheridan, Wyoming 82801
Craft Kaleidoscope, 6412 Ferguson Street, Indianapolis 46220
Dharma Trading Company, 1952 University Avenue, Berkeley, California 94704
The Golden Eye, Box 205, Chestnut Hill, Massachusetts 02167
Heads and Tails, River Forest, Illinois 60305
Lily Mills, Shelby, North Carolina 28150
Threadbenders, 2260 Como Avenue, St Paul, Minnesota 55108
The Thread Shed, 307 Freeport Road, Pittsburgh, Pennsylvania 15215

**CANADA**
Sutton Yarns, 2054 Yonge Street, Toronto, Ontario
Leonida Leatherdale Embroidery Studio, 90 East Gate, Winnipeg, Manitoba R3C2C3

# Index

Abstract 8, 18, 21, 30, 31, 33, 36, 38–42, 73–5, 80, 81, 84, 89, 92, 99–105
Aerial views 6, 38, 39, 41, 42, 129, 130
Animals 78, 107, 108, 110, 111
Arches 12, 13, 25, 32, 33, 41, 45, 59, 60, 61–71, 74, 75, 91, 94, 121, 132, 136, 137

Balustrades and bannisters 26, 27, 88, 89, 90–2, 132, 133
Beams and rafters 59, 60, 61, 62, 63, 67
Bridges 11, 14, 130–3

Castles 10, 12, 13, 15, 38, 88, 116, 118, 131, 137
Cathedrals *see* Churches
Celtic designs 105, 106
Chimneys 16, 37, 51, 87, 97, 126, 128, 134, 136
Churches and cathedrals 1, 10, 17, 22, 28, 29, 32, 33, 40, 64, 68, 69, 80–3, 106, 108, 110, 111, 113, 114, 117, 119, 131, 135, 136, 137
Columns 13, 21, 103, 135
Cottages 10, 14, 87, 122, 124, 125, 138

Dolls' house, 23, 37

Farms 10, 126
Figures and faces 10, 14, 19, 22, 37, 58, 83, 90, 94, 105, 106, 108–14
Frame 27, 59, 63, 67, 70, 79, 87, 137, 140

Gables 16, 18, 37, 50, 53, 95, 97, 98, 123
Gardens 9, 40, 63, 65, 75, 87, 140, 141
Gates 14, 25, 59, 69, 73, 74, 75, 125, 140

Interiors, 21, 37, 60–3, 67, 89, 92, 103
Islamic 39, 41, 54, 63, 64, 71, 104, 120

Lamps 24, 25, 37, 114, 115
Lighthouse 88, 127

Manor-house, 10, 14, 16, 17, 26, 27, 95, 96, 97, 125
Mills, wind and water 14, 16, 17, 88, 126

Pagodas 11, 15, 16, 121

Rafters *see* Beams

Samplers, 9, 11, 16, 17, 27
Scaffolding 57, 58, 127
Sculpture, stone and wood 10, 12, 19, 20, 21, 22, 29, 36, 65, 68, 70, 71, 78, 80, 81, 94, 98, 99, 101–15
Shops 18, 19, 77
Silhouettes 1, 25, 26, 39, 58, 61, 62, 75, 84, 89, 90, 92, 120, 126, 127, 128, 131, 141
Stained glass 61, 76, 80–4

Techniques:
   Appliqué 15, 28, 40, 44, 62, 68, 70, 119, 120, 123, 127, 128, 138
   Blackwork 28, 59, 76, 82, 135
   Canvaswork 15, 34, 35, 40, 48, 49, 57, 59, 78, 104, 123, 124
   Collage 28
   Couching, 38, 51, 113, 114
   Cross stitch 16, 17, 27, 35, 59, 123
   Cutwork 27, 55, 62, 84
   Hand-stitchery 40, 51, 54, 68, 78, 80, 119, 120, 123, 130
   Hardanger 27
   Knitting and crochet 54, 124, 127, 133, 140
   Machine embroidery 28, 40, 57, 70, 118, 128, 138, 140
   Metal thread work 13, 14, 38, 44, 57, 68, 69, 81, 113, 114, 119, 133
   Needleweaving 54, 139
   Padding 10, 15, 27, 44, 68, 69, 113, 120, 127, 133, 136, 140
   Patchwork 9, 27, 38, 40, 51, 75, 76, 78, 83, 84, 99,
   Pulled work, 59
   Quilting 27, 35, 38, 44, 45, 51, 55, 62, 74, 78, 102, 104, 114, 121, 127, 136, 138, 139
   Tiles 15, 18, 43, 52–6, 104, 136
   Timber-frame 50, 53, 60, 71, 78, 95–7, 117
   Topiary 26, 67, 124, 125
   Towns 15, 38, 123, 128, 130, 139

Villages 14, 15, 17, 38, 39, 42, 129, 139

Walls 6, 39, 43–8, 50, 51, 101, 102, 109, 131, 133, 140, 141
Water, 14, 124, 127, 128, 130, 132, 133
Wrought-iron 69, 71, 73, 74, 75, 88, 89, 114, 115